DIRECTOR'S CHOICE
NATIONAL HERITAGE INSTITUTE OF THE CZECH REPUBLIC

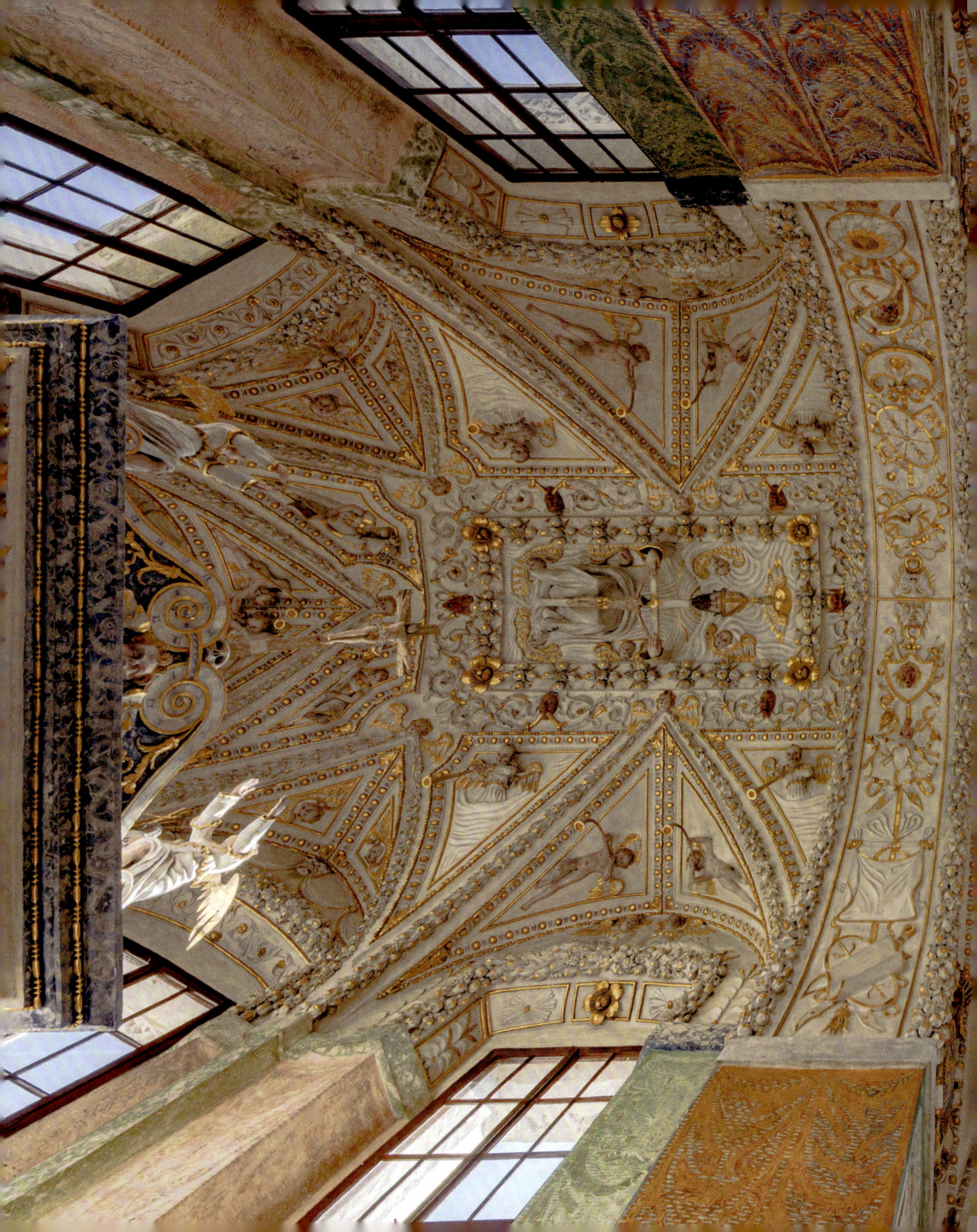

NATIONAL HERITAGE INSTITUTE OF THE CZECH REPUBLIC

Naďa Goryczková

SCALA

INTRODUCTION

The Czech Republic, thanks to its geographic position, is an important country in the heart of Europe, with a rich history and a unique range of well-preserved historical buildings set in unparalleled natural surroundings. A number of aristocratic dynasties were active in the lands of the former Czech Crown, influencing the economic, cultural and political development of the whole country. Their ancestral homes were designed not only by Czech architects and artists close to the Viennese court, but also by renowned Italian and French masters whose work aristocrats encountered on their grand tours and diplomatic missions. With the contributions of local artists and craftsmen, an unprecedented range of distinctive period architecture was created.

Due to political developments after the Second World War, the nobility were deprived of their property. The residences of a number of aristocratic families were nationalised and the centuries-old continuity of private ownership was forcibly broken.

The National Heritage Institute (Národní památkový ústav) manages these former aristocratic residences and makes them accessible to the public. The aim is to present the interiors as authentically as possible, with broad reference to the former owners and the artists and architects who left their lasting mark on these buildings.

This selection, however, is not confined to ancestral homes; it ranges far wider, encompassing many types of historical site. It includes several monastic complexes, as well as the Michal Coalmine in Ostrava, an example from the Industrial Revolution of the early twentieth century; the historic Palace Gardens below Prague Castle; and – last but not least – an outstanding monument of modern architecture: the family villa of the Brno textile manufacturer Alfred Stiassni.

The history of the buildings presented here spans the time from the fall of the Austro-Hungarian Empire until the present. This selection focuses mainly on buildings that were nationalised after the Second World War and progressively opened to the public, although we also note individual efforts to make historic buildings publicly accessible from the beginning of the nineteenth century, when some castle and château buildings which are now under the care of the National Heritage Institute were opened to the public by their then owners. The list grew longer after the First World War, with the addition of residences formerly in the possession of the Imperial House of Habsburg-Lorraine. Great changes occurred as a result of the political situation after the Second World War, when many castles and châteaux passed into the ownership of the Czechoslovak State on the basis of confiscation decrees and nationalisation after 1948. After the Velvet Revolution in 1989, a number of them were returned to the families of the original owners, but a relatively large proportion remain in the care of the National Heritage Institute. Today this amounts to more than a hundred buildings and sites, the great majority of which are open to the public. Some of them are listed as UNESCO World Heritage Sites or belong to a wider protected territory with World Heritage status.

These are remarkable works of architecture forming part of the fabric of the Czech Republic, of high architectural and art-historical value, designed and realised on a grand scale. The majority of them also feature rich period interiors with valuable historical furniture and art collections. This selection of national monuments is outstanding on a European and indeed global scale, thanks to the sheer variety of interior design within the authentic setting of historical architecture.

The range of national monuments presented here represents one of the most important assets of the Czech Republic's heritage. The exceptional quality of the interiors and art collections forms the basis of their visual appeal, while the stories of their creation make enthralling reading. It is therefore my great pleasure to present a pared-down selection of the monuments that are architecturally and typologically the most interesting. At the same time, the choice presented here will serve as an invitation to visit all the monuments under the care of the National Heritage Institute.

Dear readers, enjoy your journey through the Czech past.

Naďa Goryczková

BEČOV NAD TEPLOU

Castle

Custodian of the Romanesque Treasure

The remarkable architectural complex of gothic castle, single-wing renaissance palace and baroque château, with its adjoining garden, dominates the small town of the same name near Karlovy Vary in West Bohemia.

The fate of this once resplendent residence, shaped over the centuries by the renowned Pluh of Rabštejn, Questenberg and Kounic dynasties, was not a happy one after the Second World War. Part of the château served as the local school, and the remains of the rich interior furnishings were transferred to other heritage sites open to the public around the country. The planned restoration of this progressively deteriorating site was protracted due to a shortage of funds, and for a long time the buildings remained closed and almost forgotten by the public.

In November 1985 a dramatic find was made, unequalled in Czechoslovakia at that time. A reliquary dating from the first quarter of the thirteenth century, containing skeletal remains of Saints Maurus, John the Baptist, Apollinaris and Timothy, was discovered under the floor of the castle chapel. The reliquary, made on the instructions of the Benedictine abbey in Florennes (now in Belgium), is an exceptional work of Romanesque gilding and metalwork. In the nineteenth century it was purchased by the dukes of Beaufort-Spontin, descendants of an ancient Walloon family whose members represented Habsburg interests in the Austrian Netherlands. After the Napoleonic Wars, they resettled in Austria, and in Bohemia they purchased the Bečov estate, to which the reliquary was transferred together with other art collections.

After careful restoration, the reliquary was put on public view in 2002. Its discovery gave impetus to the systematic restoration of the site, which was honoured by the European Union in 2010 when it was selected for the prestigious Europa Nostra Award for cultural heritage. One of the outcomes of the award-winning project is the newly designed modern display area for the Saint Maurus reliquary, which is the Czech Republic's second most valuable gold relic after the Bohemian crown jewels.

BOUZOV

Castle

Fairytale stronghold of the Grand Master of the Order of Teutonic Knights

Bouzov Castle, which for nearly eight hundred years has towered majestically over the picturesque surrounding countryside, is one of the foremost examples of gothic castle architecture. At the turn of the nineteenth and twentieth centuries, it was remodelled in a spirit of Romanticism into a residence of fairytale-like appearance.

The first stronghold was founded on this site by Búz of Búzov at the turn of the thirteenth and fourteenth centuries. The castle often changed hands, and successive owners modified it in the most varied styles. In 1696 Bouzov was purchased by the Order of Teutonic Knights, and for two hundred years it served them as the economic centre of a profitable estate. The representatives of the Order visited the castle only when absolutely necessary, and therefore made no interventions affecting its appearance.

All this changed in 1894, when Archduke Eugen of Austria, Duke of Teschen, became Grand Master of the Order. As a member of the imperial family and a passionate medievalist and art lover, he decided to rebuild the castle in a spirit of historical Romanticism. He engaged the experienced Munich architect Georg von Hauberrisser, who in many respects continued in the footsteps of his predecessor who designed castles for King Ludwig II of Bavaria. The architect's plan completely ignored the existing state of evolution of the building. The castle was to be rebuilt on a grand scale inspired by the most

significant medieval monuments in Germany, France and Luxembourg. Archduke Eugen intended to make Bouzov one of the main seats of the Order, reflecting its past glory. After completion of the work, he had dozens of rare artefacts and relics brought to the castle to reflect the Order's long history, recalling the Middle Ages when the Order of Teutonic Knights was at the height of its power.

Only four years after the building was completed, the First World War broke out and the old world order collapsed. Bouzov Castle, Romanticism's swansong, remains as a unique reminder of that time.

BRNO

Villa Stiassni

Elegance of the Swing Era

IN THE TIME OF the first Czechoslovak Republic, the city of Brno, known as the 'Moravian Manchester' since the nineteenth century because of its flourishing textile industry, became a cultural and economic hub for the young country. This prosperity was soon reflected in the city's appearance, where a number of outstanding architects worked in the 1920s and 1930s in the functionalist style. The famous Hotel Avion designed by the architect Bohuslav Fuchs, for example, was built here in 1928; a year later work began on construction of the Villa Tugendhat according to plans by the architect Ludwig Mies van der Rohe, and in 2001 it was included on the UNESCO World Heritage list.

One of the best architects in Brno at that time was Ernst Wiesner – a graduate of the Vienna Academy and friend of the Brno-born architect Adolf Loos – who was renowned for his designs for villas, public buildings, industrial plants and opulent interiors of shops and cafés.

In 1927 Wiesner designed a villa for the textile factory owner Alfred Stiassni which was to be one of the largest and most luxurious in Brno. The architect designed the two-storey building on an L-shaped ground plan, with a smooth

greenish façade broken only by large window areas. In contrast with the austere modern architecture, the interiors were designed in the style of nineteenth-century rooms in a château, in accordance with the wishes of Alfred Stiassni's wife. The villa is surrounded by an extensive garden with tennis courts and a swimming pool.

Shortly before the Second World War Stiassni's Jewish family left their home and the city of Brno. The villa was confiscated by the Nazis. After the war, President Edvard Beneš was briefly based there, and subsequently it was used for official occasions by the regional authority. The owners never returned. The interiors are now open to the public, and the building also serves as a research centre for Central European modern architecture.

BUCHLOVICE

At the crossroads of history

IN THE EARLY EIGHTEENTH century *Count Jan Dětřich Petřvaldský* of Petřvald (Johann Dietrich Peterswald von Peterswald) had a baroque summer residence built with a garden around it, within sight of Buchlov Castle. According to family legend, it was a gift to his wife, Countess Anežka Eleonora, who was descended from the Italian House of Colonna. Although the architect of the château is unknown, it resembles the summer residences commissioned on the outskirts of Vienna at that time by

the most noble members of the courtly aristocracy. The symmetrically arranged château site is influenced by Italian baroque architecture, but also by French theoretical writings, whose influence is seen, in particular, in the disposition of the interiors adjoining the main hall. As was customary at the time, the owners commissioned murals and extensive stucco decorations, which were executed by Jacopo Trebelli on the ceilings and walls of the main rooms and the *sala terrena* (ground-floor hall).

In this form, the summer residence served its owners until the end of the eighteenth century, when Countess Anežka Eleonora of Petřvald decided to adapt the château interiors in the *goût grec* style according to designs by the Brno sculptor and decorative painter Ondřej Schweigl. It is likely that he also drew up the plans for the new *anglo-chinois* garden which replaced the existing baroque parterres.

The château enjoyed its greatest fame in 1908 when its then owner, Count Leopold Berchtold, arranged a meeting here between the foreign ministers of Russia and Austria-Hungary to discuss the division of their spheres of influence in the Balkans. This meeting was to be one of the inciting incidents for the First World War. The whole of Europe fixed its gaze on the elegant, newly appointed château.

Buchlovice Château is now one of the most important baroque aristocratic residences in the Czech Republic. The quality of the architecture, the extensive collections, the renown of its former owners and the importance of this château in the history of the final years of the Habsburg monarchy make it a location whose significance extends beyond the borders of the Czech lands.

ČESKÝ KRUMLOV

Castle and Château

Stately residence of the dukes of Krumlov, part of UNESCO's World Heritage

ON A ROCKY ISLAND, the South Bohemian castle and château complex of Český Krumlov towers majestically over the River Vltava and slopes gently down from its peak to the streets of the enchanting town that bears its name. The château site as a whole contains 40 buildings and palace outhouses and is one of the most extensive in Central Europe.

From the early fourteenth century, it was the seat of the foremost noble family of the Kingdom of Bohemia – the Lords of Rožmberk (known as the Lords of the Rose). Under their ownership it underwent successive adaptations which culminated in the second half of the sixteenth century with an extensive renaissance renovation. Its most conspicuous remnant is the 'Little Castle with Tower', which is the icon of the castle site and an unmissable part of the town's panorama. In the early seventeenth century ownership of the château was taken over for a short time by Emperor Rudolf II of Habsburg, from whose successor the Krumlov estate was acquired by the Eggenbergs and, after them, the Schwarzenbergs, who were the owners until the mid-twentieth century, when the castle and château were transferred to state ownership.

Each era has left an indelible mark on the château's architecture and furnishings. The Middle Ages are represented by the impressive Wenceslas Cellars (Václavské sklepy) under the fourth courtyard which served in the past as the château's technical and economic base. The pinnacle of the power and glory of the House of Rožmberk resounds through the renaissance chambers with their murals portraying Old Testament themes and the ancient Roman goddess of the harvest, Ceres, with the wine god Bacchus. A unique exhibit is the Eggenberg Golden Carriage, made in Rome in 1638 on the orders of the Krumlov ruler Johann Anton

von Eggenberg for a diplomatic mission on which he was to inform Pope Urban VIII of the election of Ferdinand III as Holy Roman Emperor. An outstanding remnant of the age of baroque château celebrations is the Masquerade Hall, richly decorated with murals by the Viennese artist Josef Lederer, which were inspired by carnival amusements and scenes from the Italian and French *commedia dell'arte*.

The château's baroque theatre, built in 1765–66, is unique in the world and has been preserved intact to this day with its original technical equipment, stage sets, theatrical wardrobe, props and archives of the period repertoire. It is therefore one of the oldest preserved theatres of château type in Central Europe, and one of the most complex preserved baroque theatres in the world.

The extensive 11-hectare garden forms part of the château site. Created in the seventeenth century on the previous baroque layout, it later underwent rococo and classicist adaptations. In the nineteenth century the garden was redesigned in the style of an English park. A dominant feature of the garden is the monumental cascade fountain with a sculptural group of the goddess Amphitrite and Tritons at its highest level. A lower level supports statues of the sea god Neptune and, opposite him, a sea nymph with a Triton. The architectural jewel of the château garden is its rococo summerhouse, Bellarie. Its halls are decorated with charming murals in rococo style by the Třeboň artist František Jakub Prokyš. The summerhouse is equipped with a 'magic table' which was lifted, fully laden with food and refreshments, from the ground-floor kitchen to the upper salon where the nobility enjoyed spending their time. A grotto with stucco decoration and murals is preserved in the basement.

Thanks to its architectural quality, cultural tradition and size, the State Castle and Château of Český Krumlov ranks among the most important historical monuments in the Central European region. Its steady structural development from the fourteenth to the nineteenth century can be seen in the original ground plan, architectural massing, interior installations and architectural detail. It is a distinctive dominant feature and one of the most important parts of the historic town centre of Český Krumlov. It gained UNESCO World Heritage status in 1992.

FRÝDLANT

Castle and Château

Ducal residence in Terra Felix – the Happy Land

IN ONE OF THE northernmost parts of the Czech Republic, the town of Frýdlant is home to an architecturally variegated complex consisting of a medieval castle and a renaissance château, which ranks among the largest and most significant ensembles of historic buildings in North Bohemia.

Frýdlant Castle was built in the mid-thirteenth century on a basalt rock washed by the River Smědá, but the Indika Tower, which rises through the castle building and forms its dominant feature, was already there some two centuries earlier; a fire that was lit on its flat roof marked an old trade route. The castle later grew up around it. After a further three hundred years, the castle was modified and rebuilt by the Bieberstein family; in 1551 it was bought by the Redern family, who added the last renaissance wing and set about extending the buildings into the surrounding area. In this way the castle on the rock was augmented with a newly built palace with a chapel dedicated to Saint Anne, as well as a large renaissance château with beautiful sgraffito decoration.

However, after 1621 Frýdlant was confiscated from the Protestant Rederns and sold to the prominent Bohemian military leader and politician Albrecht von Waldstein (Wallenstein), who gradually built a huge farm estate here. During the Thirty Years' War his farms grew to unprecedented size because they supplied his army. At that time Frýdlant became known as Terra Felix – the Happy Land.

After Duke Albrecht von Waldstein was murdered, ownership passed to the Gallas family, later Clam-Gallas, whose other possessions included the nearby Libverda Spa. In 1801 the castle was opened to spa guests and others who wished to visit – an unusual decision for those times. As a result, Frýdlant became the earliest castle museum in Central Europe.

HLUBOKÁ NAD VLTAVOU

Château

The Schwarzenbergs' family seat

WITH ITS DISTINCTIVE CHARACTER, well-preserved collection of original furniture and large park, Hluboká Château in South Bohemia stands out as one of Europe's most romantic sites. Its history extends far further back than its present form. Originally a thirteenth-century watchkeeping castle stood here; as property of the Bohemian kings, it was repeatedly expanded. Under the Lords of Hradec, the castle was transformed into an imposing renaissance château. Later, in 1661, it was bought by Johann Adolf I von Schwarzenberg, and it remained in this family's possession until it was nationalised in 1947.

The château underwent its last major change around the mid-nineteenth century, when Prince Johann Adolf II had it converted to neo-gothic style. The appearance of the château site including the park and the surrounding landscape was inspired by his journeys to Great Britain, where he attended the coronation of Queen Victoria in 1838. As an honorary diplomat of the Habsburg monarchy, he travelled to the coronation with his wife, Princess Eleonora, whose ideas were influential in shaping the appearance of the château. Hluboká soon became the seat of the Schwarzenberg family.

The white façade, battlements and towers were intended to give the château a medieval appearance, recalling the antiquity and nobility of the House of Schwarzenberg. The owners also devoted considerable attention to furnishing the state rooms on the main floor. The collection of tapestries and the château library are famous. The accommodation provided every comfort available to the aristocratic elites of the second half of the nineteenth century – hot-air heating, hydraulic lifts, flushing toilets and, from 1909, electricity.

Together with the 60-acre English park which surrounds the château, Hloboká nad Vltavou is one of the most romantic château sites in Bohemia and reveals a great deal about the taste and prominent role of the House of Schwarzenberg.

HRADEC NAD MORAVICÍ

Château

Residence of cosmopolitan princes

THE LARGE CHÂTEAU COMPLEX in Hradec nad Moravicí, with its Empire and neo-gothic architecture, is surrounded by a naturally landscaped park which is outstanding in its composition and variety of trees. The site ranks among the largest and most impressive in the Moravian-Silesian Region; it owes its current appearance to alterations undertaken in the early nineteenth century by the princely Lichnowsky-Woschütz family, who worked skilfully as negotiators between Vienna and Berlin in the official and diplomatic services of the Austrian Habsburgs and the Prussian Hohenzollerns. Their growing social status was manifested in 1778 by their purchase of the Hradec nad Moravicí estate and large-scale alterations to the residence there. On a long rocky promontory overlooking the River Moravice, on the site of the gothic castle of the Přemyslid king Ottokar II of Bohemia, the elegant building known as the White

Castle took shape in the nineteenth century, with neo-classical alterations to the façades, and with the later additions of a neo-gothic connecting section in the courtyard and the separately standing White Tower.

The area of the site nearly doubled with the construction of the neo-gothic Red Castle with its fairfaced brickwork, the imposing tower-like entrance gate and the clocktower, stables and coach-houses. To complete the surroundings a large, naturally landscaped park was created, with several viewing points. The striking appearance of the princely residence was more than matched by the Lichnowkys' personal contacts with the leading figures in the Austrian and German cultural, artistic and political spheres. Among those who stayed at the château were the composers Ludwig van Beethoven and Franz Liszt, the German chancellor Otto von Bismarck, the poet Rainer Maria Rilke and the artist Oskar Kokoschka, whose portrait of Princess Mechtilde Lichnowsky deserves its place as one of the most valuable works in the National Heritage Institute's collections.

HRÁDEK U NECHANIC

Château

A piece of England in Bohemia

HRÁDEK U NECHANIC IN East Bohemia is a perfectly preserved château site in the romantic gothic style of the mid-nineteenth century. As such, it is one of the foremost examples of romantic architecture in the Czech lands, realised in the style of English gothic.

The château was built in 1839–57 by Franz Ernst, Count of Harrach, as a summer hunting seat for the prominent Harrach dynasty of counts. A plan drawn up by the English architect Edward Buckton Lamb in the Tudor gothic style served as a model for the building. The château is constructed on a ground plan resembling a widely open letter 'V', with a number of projecting sections that give it a unique appearance. Particularly distinctive is its silhouette, richly embellished with battlements and other fortress-like elements.

The construction work was directed by the eminent Austrian architect Karl Fischer, who revised the plans and also designed the interior

décor for the château. In addition to the furnishings, which were created mainly by local craftsmen, many antiques were brought to the château, especially from Italy and Austria. In many cases these were entire portals, ceilings or the complete furnishing of a room. In 1844, while the château was under construction, the garden designer L. Krüger adapted part of the surrounding wood as a country park; in other parts of the wood, a game park and pheasantry were created.

In view of its relatively short history as one of the most recently built châteaux in the Czech Republic, it is unique in the Czech context in that until 1945, when it was transferred to the state, it was owned by only one family, namely the family that commissioned its construction, the Harrachs. For this reason, too, the château exhibition presented for visitors is now mainly a display of the domestic setting, taste and lifestyle of this aristocratic family in the second half of the nineteenth century.

JAROMĚŘICE NAD ROKYTNOU

Elegant baroque residence in the style of Versailles

THE IMPOSING COMPLEX OF château and sacral architecture in Jaroměřice nad Rokytnou, South Moravia, together with its ornamental garden and park, is one of the largest sites of the High Baroque in the Czech Republic and Europe as a whole, and stands out as an exceptionally impressive sight.

The extensive baroque château and the Church of St Margaret, with its two towers, were commissioned by the art-loving Johann Adam, Count of

Questenberg, according to a plan by the Austrian master builder Jakob Prandtauer, as a renovation of the original family seat. The master builder Domenico d'Angeli of Znojmo and many other masters took part in the construction, which was carried out mainly in 1710–37. At the same time, the château garden was created in the French style with the assistance of the Viennese architect Jean Trehet.

Count Questenberg dedicated most of his life to the construction of the Jaroměřice residence. In accordance with his wishes, two large halls were built in the château – a hall with portraits of his ancestors and a ballroom painted with chinoiserie and historicising motifs – as well as a library, garden hall, Roman baths, a hall for ball games, and the château's own opera hall, since he was a devotee and patron of opera. He was an outstanding musician himself, a lutenist, and he arranged musical and operatic events at Jaroměřice for many high-born guests. The performances that took place in the château included, in 1730, the premiere of the first Czech opera, *The Origins of Jaroměřice*, by the composer and kapellmeister to the Questenbergs, František Václav Míča.

The furniture in the count's chambers includes a remarkable chinoiserie cabinet, preserved intact to this day, decorated by the *lacca povera* technique with flower motifs in découpage. This, together with the large halls, *sala terrena* (ground-floor hall) and baths, creates an exceptionally authentic interior in this château which, thanks to its grand baroque conception, has earned the nickname 'the Moravian Versailles'.

JINDŘICHŮV HRADEC

Castle and Château

Medieval and renaissance residence of Czech grandees

THE CASTLE AND CHÂTEAU complex in Jindřichův Hradec is one of the largest heritage sites in the Czech Republic. Together with the neighbouring historic town, the imposing ensemble of castle and château buildings forms a harmonious whole, whose historic character and architectural heritage are united in one of the country's oldest urban conservation areas.

The château site is first mentioned in written sources in 1220 as a stone castle owned by the Lords of Hradec, who influenced the politics and culture of the Czech lands for centuries. From the thirteenth to the fifteenth century, the site retained a number of unique interiors including a room with paintings dating from 1338 depicting the legend of Saint George, the private chapel of Henry IV of Hradec and the medieval Black Kitchen.

The grandest rebuilding of the site took place in the second half of the sixteenth century under the Lords of Hradec, who transformed the castle into a magnificent renaissance château according to a plan by the Italian architect Baldassare Maggi of Arogna. Outstanding features remaining from that renovation are the high loggias in the main courtyard and especially the Rondel – a garden pavilion with excellent stucco and painted decoration, which ranks among the most delightful central buildings of the Bohemian renaissance.

The appearance and furnishing of the château also show the influence of the noble Czernin family, who inherited it in the late seventeenth century and built their family museum here. The château belonged to them until 1945, when it was expropriated by the state. From that time onwards the condition of the site progressively deteriorated, and some buildings were on the verge of collapse. A reconstruction programme was therefore launched in 1976 and continued for nearly ten years; as a result, the site was preserved and was opened to the public in 1993. To this day we can admire the impressive architecture of Jindřichův Hradec Château reflected in Lake Vajgar.

# KARLŠTEJN
Castle

Treasury for the imperial Crown Jewels

KARLŠTEJN OCCUPIES THE MOST important place among the medieval royal residences of the Kingdom of Bohemia, and is still regarded as one of the symbols of Czech statehood. It is also a historic residence associated with the history of the Holy Roman Empire.

The imposing castle was founded in 1348 by the Czech king and Holy Roman Emperor Charles IV of Luxembourg, as a symbol of his state's ambitions and also, after his election as emperor, as a magnificently decorated stronghold to store the badges of imperial power: the imperial reliquaries and crown. The architecture in its hierarchical arrangement from the lowest to the highest parts of the castle complex reflects the founder's religious and philosophical ideas. Its highest point is the castle's Great Tower with the Chapel of the Holy Cross, alluding to the heavenly Jerusalem. The chapel is one of the most remarkably preserved sacral spaces of medieval Europe. The lower part of its interior walls is decorated with semiprecious stones; its vaulted ceiling is gilded and decorated with stars, moon and sun made of Venetian glass. The walls are covered with 129 panel paintings by Master Theodoric dating from the fourteenth century, portraying saints, angels and prophets. Behind a gilded lattice partition there is an altar triptych by the Italian painter Tommaso da Modena, as well as a niche box for storing the imperial treasure and later the Bohemian Crown Jewels. The lower parts of the castle include the Marian Tower with the Chapel of the Virgin Mary and the Chapel of St Catherine and, further down, the royal palace with the Manský Hall, the Chapel of St Nicholas and the imperial chambers. A renaissance burgrave house stands in the lower courtyard.

Although the castle was adapted in neo-gothic style by the architect Josef Mocker in the nineteenth century and the exterior partly lost its authentic appearance, the exceptionally valuable artistic furnishings make Karlštejn one of the most precious historical buildings in the country and a pinnacle of medieval art.

KLADRUBY

Monastery

Ancient seat of the Benedictines

KLADRUBY MONASTERY WITH THE Church of the Assumption of the Virgin Mary represents the high point of the baroque gothic style in Bohemia, and serves as a reminder of the exceptional creative ability of the foremost representative of the radical baroque style, the architect Jan Blažej Santini-Aichel. The monastery buildings also contain valuable elements of other stylistic periods, so that they form a record of continuity and confirm the fact that the West Bohemian seat of the Benedictines was for centuries an important religious, economic and cultural centre for the entire region.

The history of the monastery dates from 1115, when it was built on the orders of the Přemyslid prince Vladislaus I for the Benedictine Order,

to support the colonisation of the sparsely populated border region in the west of Bohemia. The first early medieval complex of buildings was completed in 1233, concurrently with the triple-nave basilica. In the thirteenth and fourteenth centuries, Kladruby Monastery was one of the largest communities in the Bohemian province of the Benedictines. Later, the flourishing monastery was plundered by the Hussites, and was not renovated until the second half of the seventeenth century, when the monastery and the Church of the Assumption of the Virgin Mary were repaired and a new prelate's residence was built.

The monastery enjoyed its greatest flowering under Abbott Maurus Fintzgut, who had the monastery church rebuilt in 1712–26 according to a plan by Jan Blažej Santini-Aichel, in the baroque gothic style. The main nave, 86 metres long, makes the Kladruby church the third largest in Bohemia. The monumental building is topped by a dome with a gilded Marian crown. Santini designed not only the building, but also parts of the interior, including the main altar, the pulpit and the organ cases. For the decorative work he collaborated with some of the greatest Central European artists of his time, such as the sculptor and woodcarver Matthias Bernard Braun and the Bavarian painter Cosmas Damian Asam. The preserved buildings and interiors are testimony to the perfect unity of the architecture with its religious contents.

KONOPIŠTĚ

Château

Residence of the heir to the imperial throne

THE MOST IMPORTANT CHAPTER in the history of Konopiště Château played out at the turn of the nineteenth and twentieth centuries, when it became the favourite country seat of the heir to the throne, Archduke Franz Ferdinand of Austria-Este. The original medieval castle was rebuilt many times in the Renaissance and Baroque periods, and each of these stages left its mark. The archduke bought the château with its estate and renowned hunting lodges in 1887 and had it rebuilt in romantic style by the architect Josef Mocker. A rose garden, a greenhouse for exotic plants and a romantic-style park were created at the château.

The archduke was heir to the last duke of Modena from the Habsburg-Lorraine branch of the family, and transferred to Konopiště the valuable Modena collections that had been taken to Austria at the time of the unification of Italy. The château became a luxurious residence with modern furnishings and major collections of paintings by Italian masters, a collection of rare renaissance and early baroque cabinets, and the renowned armoury of the dukes of Este. It also served as the seat of the archduke's family because in 1900 he married Sophie Chotek, who was descended from a family which, though ancient, was of inferior rank, bearing the title of count, and he gained the ruling Austrian emperor's approval for this marriage only at the cost of excluding his future heirs from succession to the throne.

At Konopiště, the archduke had the rooms arranged for his family in a more modern, private style. Since he and his wife were murdered in Sarajevo in 1914, these rooms have remained almost unchanged to this day. They are on view together with the reception rooms, the Este collections, the archduke's collection of paintings of Saint George and his hunting trophies. Visitors to the château therefore have a unique opportunity to see the residence of the heir to the imperial throne in an authentic state of preservation, as if he left the château only yesterday.

KROMĚŘÍŽ
Flower Garden

Baroque Elysium

THE FLOWER GARDEN, ONE of the major Central European garden projects of the Early Baroque, is inseparably linked with its creator, Karl II von Liechtenstein-Kastelkorn, Bishop of Olomouc. During his studies, this magnate and intellectual travelled through Germany and Italy, where he came to know the cities that were the seats of the most prominent secular and ecclesiastical princes, and the refined lifestyle of their rulers. He decided to bring all this to the episcopal city of Kroměříž, which he intended to make the centre for his possessions and power. After 1664, when he rose to the episcopal throne, he began with an extensive baroque reconstruction of the château and town, for which he engaged the imperial architect Filiberto Lucchese and a number of other, mainly Italian artists working on stonework, statues, paintings and stucco. Thanks to the bishop's wide-ranging activity as a patron and collector, one of Titian's most famous paintings, *Apollo and Marsyas*, and many other masterpieces came to Moravia, and are now kept in the collections of the Olomouc Archdiocese.

The bishop's endeavours in Kroměříž reached their artistic peak with the Flower Garden or Libosad (pleasure garden), laid out in 1665 on the site of the old orchard outside the city walls. He devoted the utmost care to this project and called on the assistance of the best available expert, the imperial architect Filiberto Lucchese. After his death the garden was taken over in 1666 by another architect in the imperial service, Giovanni Pietro Tencalla.

In many ways the garden was to resemble the major garden projects in Italy, France and Germany, which included, for example, the garden of the Villa d'Este in Tivoli, the garden of the elector's residence in Munich and the garden of the Salzburg archbishops' country residence at Hellbrunn. The refined taste exemplified in the Italian gardens, which was inspired by the artistic principles of mannerism, was complemented

at Kroměříž by the latest French influences manifested in the magnificent garden projects of André Le Nôtre at Versailles, and the Château de Vaux-le-Vicomte.

The site of the Flower Garden, laid out on an oblong ground plan, consists of the flower garden itself and the adjacent orchard. While the former comprises tall trimmed bushes, a maze and parterres, the latter consists of well-pruned trees, water features, small hills overgrown with strawberry plants, the rabbit hill, the aviary, greenhouses and the Dutch Garden and Orange Garden. On its north side the garden is bounded by a magnificent colonnade almost 250 metres long, with mythological statues carved by the bishop's court sculptors Michal Mandík and Michael Zürn. The artists took the patterns for the statues from prints depicting the famous Roman garden of the Villa Doria Pamphili, which the Kroměříž project was to rival. The summerhouse – the 'Lusthaus', also known as the Rotunda –

is built on a central ground plan in the middle of the clusters of trees (bosquets), according to a plan by Pietro Tencalla. It is embellished inside with magnificent stucco and painted decorations, on which the stucco modeller Quirico Catelli and the painter Giacomo Tencalla collaborated.

In the late eighteenth century the Flower Garden was outshone by the newly built *anglo-chinois* park under the château. The Flower Garden became merely a storage area for flowers. In the 1840s Empire-style greenhouses and other buildings were added, so that the baroque layout of the garden is preserved to this day.

In Kroměříž, which is known as 'the Athens of Haná' because of its unique range of architectural monuments and gardens, the magnificence of the Flower Garden is convincing evidence of how the richest aristocrats of the time lavished attention on their garden projects. In view of its significance the Flower Garden, together with the château and adjoining Château Garden, was entered on the UNESCO World Heritage list in 1998.

KŘIVOKLÁT

A royal castle in the middle of a hunting forest

Křivoklát Castle is one of the best-known and oldest royal castles in Bohemia. The present appearance of this architecturally and historically outstanding complex, with its surviving early gothic two-part layout and late gothic mass composition, is the result of a complex constructional evolution.

The castle, with its high cylindrical tower and palace with a chapel, was built in the thirteenth century in the middle of a large hunting ground of the Bohemian kings, on the site of an earlier, probably wooden castle first mentioned in 1100. It became the favourite hunting spot for Bohemian kings of the Přemyslid and Luxembourg dynasties. In the fifteenth century King Ladislaus Jagiellon had the castle rebuilt in late gothic style. The Royal Hall was created here – the largest gothic interior after the Vladislav Hall in Prague Castle. The castle chapel was fitted out with mesh vaulting, sedilia (seating), statues of the apostles and an altarpiece made before 490, with a central carving of the Coronation of the Virgin and painted wings with Marian scenes and saints. The paintings are the work of the Master of the Křivoklát Altar and are important evidence of the influence of Dutch art in the Czech lands, mediated by the work of Rhineland artists.

Under Habsburg ownership the castle served both as a state prison and as a refuge. In the seventeenth century it passed into the ownership of aristocratic families; the last of these was the House of Fürstenberg. While in their possession the castle was damaged by fire in 1826, and was restored in romantic style by the architects Josef Mocker and

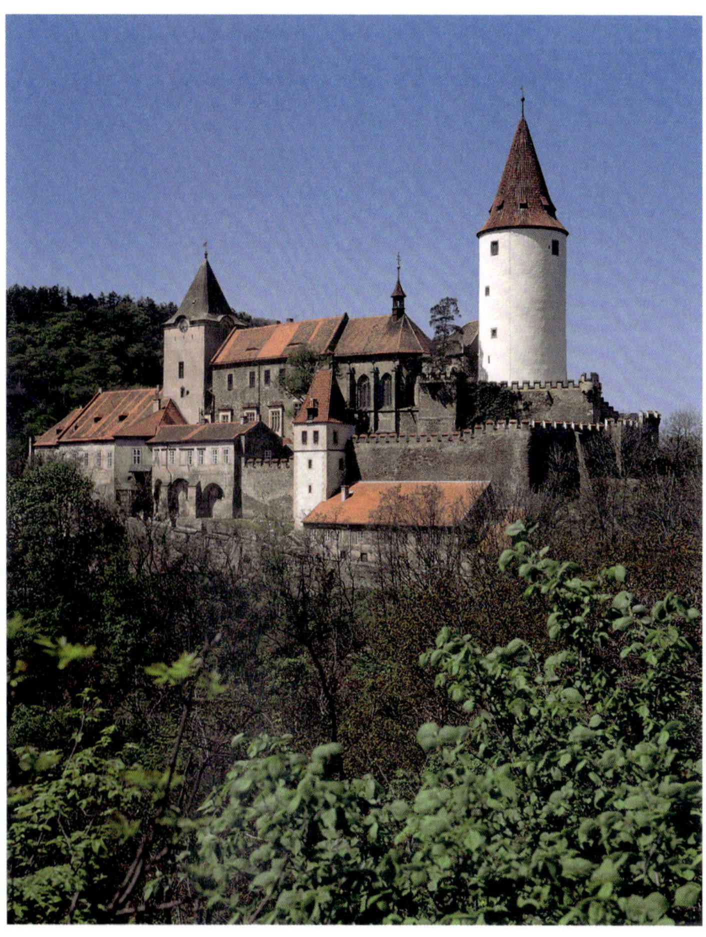

Kamil Hilbert at the turn of the nineteenth and twentieth centuries. In this way it took shape as a family museum.

Many parts of this renowned royal castle – especially the Royal Hall, Knights' Hall, chapel, ground-floor hall and passageway with early medieval sedilia – have largely retained their authentic medieval appearance, making this castle a uniquely well-preserved representative seat of the Bohemian kings.

KUKS

Hospital

Mysterious baroque hospital – between Virtues and Vices

The Kuks Hospital in East Bohemia is a unique complex of baroque spas and hospitals. It retains its value primarily as an urban complex which is evidence of the mature intellectual and artistic level of the High Baroque era.

This was perfectly embodied in the person of the politician, publisher and patron of the arts Count Franz Anton von Sporck, who founded the Kuks Hospital in the early eighteenth century as a place of rest for ex-soldiers. It was laid down in the founding document that the hospital was intended for a hundred old men in need of care, who would be looked after by the Brothers of Mercy. It was the most generous institute of its kind in Late Baroque Bohemia, and was also generously conceived from an artistic point of view. World-renowned artists contributed to the appearance of the baroque complex at Kuks – especially the architect Giovanni Battista Alliprandi and the sculptor Matthias Bernard Braun, who in 1718–20 created allegorical statues of the Virtues and Vices which are placed on the terrace in front of the hospital, perfectly underscoring the grandeur of the building. The dominant feature of the site is the renowned Holy Trinity Church, constructed on a ground plan of extended octagonal shape. In addition, one of the oldest baroque pharmacies and the Czech Republic's only pharmaceutical museum are located here.

The hospital no longer serves its original purpose, but visitors can acquaint themselves with its remarkable history on several sightseeing tours. Since the entire site underwent a major renovation in 2013–15, for which it received a number of prestigious awards, it has functioned not only as a publicly accessible historical monument, but also as an important cultural and educational centre for the region, and as the location for many cultural activities.

KYNŽVART
Castle

Summer residence of Chancellor Metternich

IN THE 1820S AND 1830S Prince Klemens Wenzel Lothar von Metternich-Winneburg, state chancellor of the Habsburg Monarchy, commissioned a neoclassical residence to be built in Kynžvart, West Bohemia, in place of the original baroque château. The rebuilding was entrusted to Pietro Nobile, a Vienna architect of Italian origin, who created a symmetrical structure with a central Great Hall surrounded by rooms and apartments, a wing with guest rooms and an opposite wing with a chapel, the chancellor's cabinet of curiosities and a library. With its large collection of incunabula, this library is one of the most important aristocratic libraries in the Czech Republic.

The château park dating from the same time, with its romantic-style pavilions and exotic plants, was designed by the Viennese court gardener Johann Michael Riedel. In the elegant interiors, decorated in the restrained style of late Central European neoclassicism, the chancellor gathered his notable collections and famous gifts from European rulers and other personalities, which he received as the foremost architect of

European policy who presided over the ending of the Napoleonic Wars at the Congress of Vienna 1814–15.

In the early twentieth century valuable paintings, marble sculptures and decorative vases were also brought here from the chancellor's collections in Vienna, including sculptures by Berthel Thorvaldsen and works of other artists which remain in the Great Hall. Many of these objects were assigned to special rooms in the cabinet of curiosities, where the chancellor's collections are displayed to this day.

The château site as a whole is the only complete example of an impressive country residence in the late Viennese classicist and Empire styles in the Czech lands. At the same time it provided a record of the lifestyle and ambitions of Chancellor Metternich as the foremost personality at the top level of European politics at the time. For this reason the château was entered on the list of European Heritage Label sites in 2019.

LEDNICE

Romantic princely residence in a grandly landscaped setting, under UNESCO protection

WHEN EMPEROR LEOPOLD I of Habsburg visited Moravia in 1672, he expressed an interest in seeing the château of Prince Karl Eusebius von Liechtenstein in Lednice. The sovereign was enraptured by the beauty of what he saw and he became one of the most famous visitors, among other personalities such as King Ferdinand I of Naples, the German chancellor Otto von Bismarck and Prince Arthur of England. The Green Heart of Europe, as the château garden and landscaped country around Lednice are often called, covers 200 square kilometres and ranks among the largest landscaped areas in Europe.

In Lednice in the early 1600s Prince Karl I of Liechtenstein commissioned a renaissance villa inspired by the Palladian villas around Vicenza and Venice. The building, on a simple ground plan, was surrounded by an Italian garden with parterres and water features, followed by a hunting ground in the nearby floodplain meadows. The next prince, Karl Eusebius, also devoted his attention to the garden, converting the villa into a château, and, with the assistance of the Italian gardener Camino Manini, he created one of the most remarkable gardens in Europe, with an orangery that was equally famous. Then, under Prince Johann Adam Andreas I von Liechtenstein, the extensive baroque stables and riding school were created at Lednice, both according to a plan by the imperial architect Johann Bernhard Fischer von Erlach.

The period of the greatest changes to Lednice began in the late eighteenth century, when these extensive properties

were in the hands of Prince Aloys I von Liechtenstein, a passionate
Anglophile, Freemason and patron of Mozart and many other artists.
He converted the baroque garden into a country park with a number of
small buildings, constructed according to a plan by the court architect
Josef Hardtmuth. At the turn of the eighteenth and nineteenth centuries
a magnificent minaret was erected here on the prince's instructions,
as a symbol for the whole of Lednice. Its exotic tower, towering over
exotic trees, served as a viewing point over the entire landscaped area.

In addition to the minaret, Hardtmuth designed several other buildings in the park and its surroundings: the Janohrad ('John's Castle') – an artificial ruin reminiscent of medieval castles – and a mock ruin of an ancient aqueduct, as well as Turkish baths and an obelisk.

Yet another prince, Johann I, continued with the extension of the park and surrounding landscaped country, drawing upon the skills of (in addition to Hardtmuth) the architects Josef Kornhäusel and Josef Franz Engel, who built the Lakeside Mansion, Temple of Apollo, Borderland Château and Temple of the Three Graces near Lednice.

Alterations were made in a spirit of Romanticism by the next owner of Lednice, Prince Aloys II, who had sufficient means to undertake what was until then the most extensive conversion of the château, in the style of international neo-gothic. The previously baroque façades of the château

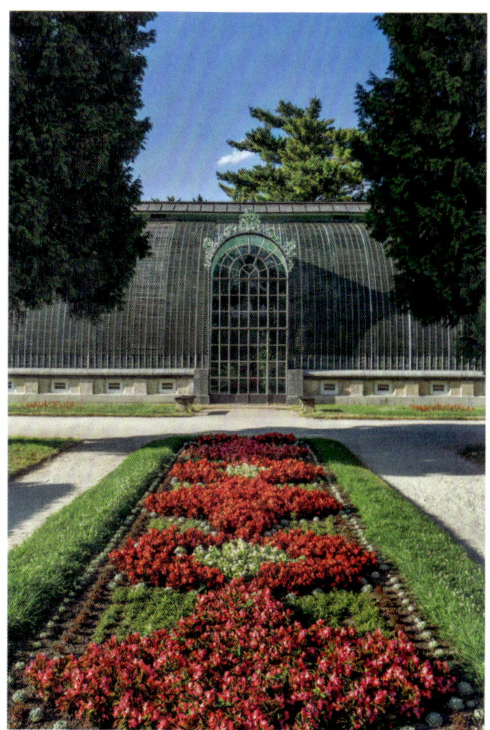

were embellished in the mid-nineteenth century with battlements, oriel windows, towers, pinnacles, gargoyles and windows with broken arches, turning Lednice into a romantic dream.

The court architect Georg Wingelmüller also undertook most of the interior design of the château with the collaboration of renowned Viennese furniture companies. The main salons of the château, fitted out with coffered ceilings, wood panelling and rare tapestries, were equipped with every modern comfort – bathrooms, hot-air heating and lifts. Work on the château was followed by a gigantic greenhouse with a cast-iron frame, designed in line with the trends of the British Industrial Revolution.

In 1996 this romantic-style residence, with a neo-baroque garden parterre added in the early twentieth century, was placed on the UNESCO World Heritage list, complete with the extensive landscaped cultural area and also including Valtice Château and other outstanding architectural monuments. It has long been one of the most-visited historical sites in the Czech Republic.

LITOMYŠL
Château

A palace in Italian renaissance style, part of UNESCO World Heritage

THE CHÂTEAU IN LITOMYŠL provides a valuable record of the Italian type of arcaded château. In its uniquely well-preserved entirety, it perfectly exemplifies a Central European aristocratic residence of the Renaissance era which has maintained its unique character despite subsequent changes in line with new movements in art.

The château lies at an important transport node – on the main road between Bohemia and Moravia, on the site of an original fortified settlement. The château itself, designed by the Italian architect Giovanni Battista Aostalli de Sala, was built in the 1560s–80s by the Highest Chancellor of the Kingdom of Bohemia, Vratislav II of Pernštejn, for his wife, Maria Manrique de Lara. It is a four-winged, three-storey building with an asymmetrical layout, constructed on an almost square ground

plan with a central courtyard. The external façades of the château are not divided into sections, but are embellished with rich sgraffito decorations and shield designs incorporated into the architecture, giving the exterior of the château an utterly distinctive appearance.

The Pernštejns' spectacular residence was later modified in baroque and classicist style by subsequent owners – the families of Count Trauttmansdorff and Count Waldstein – with the assistance of leading baroque artists. No less interesting is the artistic mark left on Litomyšl by its last owners, the Princes of Thurn and Taxis.

A striking element of the château interior is the exceptionally well-preserved theatre of the Waldstein family, dating from 1797. This is the second oldest theatre in the Czech Republic, which has retained more than 20 of its original stage sets designed by Josef Platzer. He was a famous creator of theatre scenery for the Vienna court theatre and provided the backdrop, for example, for the Prague premiere of Mozart's opera *Don Giovanni* in the Estates Theatre (Stavovské divadlo).

The château has other richly furnished and well-preserved interiors, which are essentially renaissance, with rich late baroque and neoclassical decoration in the form of elaborate plasterwork and wall and ceiling paintings. The largest area of the château's displays is devoted to the penultimate generation of Waldsteins at Litomyšl, especially Anton I von Waldstein-Wartenberg. He commissioned, among other things, a French garden

with a summerhouse on the west side of the château. The painted decoration of the summerhouse in Egyptian style reflects the fashion of the time, following Napoleon's campaign in Egypt. The landscaped country park also owes its appearance to those times; in its south-western part, Anton I von Waldstein-Wartenberg had a memorial with a statue of a lion erected in honour of his younger brother Franz, who died in the Napoleonic Wars. In the château interiors, one's attention is drawn, in particular, to the family's love of horse-breeding, as reflected in the large paintings in the Great Dining Hall; and to Prince Eugene of Savoy, an eminent Habsburg military leader and politician, who is portrayed in oil paintings in the billiard room. Also noteworthy are the château interiors dating from the turn of the nineteenth and twentieth centuries, when the château was owned by the Princely House of Thurn and Taxis of Regensburg, who were famed for operating a postal service and were present at the start of the most famous horse race in Bohemia – the Grand Pardubice Steeplechase. In 1889 the Thurn and Taxis family hosted the emperor himself, Franz Joseph I, at the château, as commemorated in the apartment where he stayed during his five-day visit. The château site also includes the buildings of the former brewery, where the word-renowned composer Bedřich Smetana was born in 1824.

With its unique architecture, its original exterior preserved in authentic form and its impressive interiors, the château at Litomyšl represents an outstandingly instructive example of a Central European aristocratic residence in renaissance style. It was therefore added to the UNESCO World Heritage List in 1999.

LYSICE

Château

All European history in one place

AT FIRST GLANCE, THE baroque château of Lysice in the town of the same name, at the foot of the Bohemian-Moravian Highlands, does not catch the eye with flamboyant splendour or architectural grandeur, but visitors are won over by its intimacy and charm, its rich interiors and unique garden. The first aristocratic residence in Lysice was founded by the Lords of Kunštát, who built a small water castle, which was later converted into a renaissance château. The château owes its baroque appearance, which it has retained to this day, to Count Anton Amatus Serényi of Lysice, who enjoyed the château mainly for its superb terraced garden with a viewing gallery and the *sala terrena*.

The château's most significant period is associated with the family of Counts Dubský von Třebomyslice, who inherited the château and estate in the early 1800s. In the mid-nineteenth century the château underwent alterations in a historicist style according to the instructions of the owner, Count Emanuel Dubský. It gained an elegant staircase and a number of stylish interiors furnished in the rococo revival manner and a spirit of historicism.

In the nineteenth century the château was a vibrant hub of social life which included not only the Count's immediate family, but their relative the Austrian writer Marie Ebner von Eschenbach and the Slovenian poet France Prešeren. Above all, it was Emanuel Dubský's son, Count Erwin Dubský, a high-ranking officer in the Austrian Navy, who brought fame to Lysice Château. On his travels around the world he brought extensive oriental collections to the château, as well as a unique collection of some of the earliest photographs taken in Japan, comparable with only a few collections of similar material around the world.

This romantic château, with its superb interiors, collections and the famous colonnaded promenade around the garden's enchanting parterre, is one of the most perfect examples of a nineteenth-century residence of the Moravian nobility.

MNICHOVO HRADIŠTĚ

Château

The life of a glorious château in the eighteenth century

MNICHOVO HRADIŠTĚ CHÂTEAU IN the town of the same name in Central Bohemia is a valuable example of a high baroque architectural complex within the territory of the Czech Republic. During the first third of the seventeenth century the original renaissance château came into the possession of the powerful commander and generalissimo of the Imperial Army, Albrecht von Waldstein, whose large estate at Mnichovo Hradiště passed to his cousin Count Maximilian von Waldstein and his descendants. At the turn of the seventeenth and eighteenth centuries the château was rebuilt by the Italian architects and builders Marc Antonio Canevalle and Nicollo Raimondi as an impressive baroque residence with a French garden, Capuchin monastery, church and Chapel of St Anne. In 1709–10 the development of the château site was completed with the addition of auxiliary buildings – stables, riding schools, coach houses and the *sala terrena.*

In the second half of the eighteenth century the Waldstein court painter Georg Hisler decorated the walls of the salons on the main floor with murals. These showed Venetian and Neapolitan vistas in the Italian Room, hunting scenes in the Hunting Room and portraits of Countess Sophie von Waldstein in the Ladies' Salon. A picture room was also created at that time, to display 111 paintings by Dutch, Italian and Central European artists of the seventeenth and eighteenth centuries. These interiors are complemented by rooms with older decorations, a large salon filled with paintings of the countryside around the château, a room housing gilded stucco medallions and a baroque chapel. The château theatre, with a collection of scenery and costumes, has been preserved since the early nineteenth century. Equally valuable is the large portrait gallery of the Waldstein dynasty, including portraits of Count Albrecht von Waldstein, who is buried here in the Chapel of St Anne, and his descendants. The château remained in the possession of this ancient Czech aristocratic family until 1946; Mnichovo Hradiště was therefore the centre of the Waldstein estate for more than three centuries.

NÁMĚŠŤ NAD OSLAVOU

Château

Music and a love of books

THE MAGNIFICENT ARCHITECTURE of the stately residence at Náměšť nad Oslavou is undoubtedly one of the most outstanding examples of renaissance building in Moravia. The château was built in the second half of the sixteenth century in a conversion of the former medieval castle on a rocky promontory above the River Oslava. The rebuilding was probably initiated by the foremost Moravian nobleman John the Elder of Žerotín, who was inspired by the renaissance architecture which he encountered when staying in Italy. Among the renaissance alterations, it is particularly the inner arcaded courtyard, the entrance portals and the richly decorated oriel at the corner of the palace that

have been preserved. In the ensuing centuries, the inner and outer areas underwent a number of alterations; the most valuable of these include the richly decorated interiors of the château's baroque chapel and the library with its fresco decoration by the Italian-Swiss painter Carpoforo Tencalla.

In 1752 the estate with the château was acquired by Count Friedrich Wilhelm von Haugwitz, who was renowned as, among other things, a patron of music, a collector of the works of George Frideric Handel and a close friend of the composer and imperial kapellmeister Antonio Salieri. During his life Náměšť became a hub of musical culture, as exemplified by many notable performances given by the château's own musical ensemble, which was unique for that time.

Although the château was nationalised after the Second World War, it soon gained a new and useful function and status when it was chosen as the summer residence of the Czechoslovak president Edvard Beneš during his visits to Moravia. The château is especially celebrated to this day for its musical past and present. Regular concerts of classical music and modern genres continue the cultural legacy of the former owners, the aristocratic Haugwitz dynasty, and confirm the position of Náměšť Château as a centre for music.

OPOČNO

Château

Renaissance treasure house in East Bohemia

OPOČNO IS ONE OF the oldest aristocratic seats in East Bohemia; the first mention of it dates to 1068 in the *Chronicle of the Czechs* (Chronicle of Cosmas). At first a fortress on the trade route to Poland stood on this site, then a gothic watchtower castle, but the most glorious period began under the rule of the noble House of Trček of Lipa. The Lords of Lipa, influenced by the Italian renaissance, commenced the construction of a magnificent renaissance site in 1560, giving today's château its characteristic arcades. Successive additions to the site were a renaissance summerhouse and hall for ball games, and the church also underwent alteration. The Trček family died out during the Thirty Years' War and their property was confiscated by the emperor, who sold it to his field marshal Rudolf von Colloredo.

The originally Italian family Colloredo, later Colloredo-Mannsfeld, owned the Opočno Château for a further three hundred years and made additional alterations to it. Under their ownership an English park was laid out under the château, with valuable trees, waterfalls, pavilions and a palm house. The most recent alterations were carried out in the early twentieth century, when the château became a comfortable family residence. At the end of the nineteenth century the Colloredo-Mannsfeld family decided to gather their rare collections at Opočno. A unique collection of Italian and Neapolitan

baroque paintings was formed here, including works by Giacomo del Po and Andrea Vaccaro, an armoury containing more than 2,500 firearms and cutting weapons (making it one of the most important collections of historical weapons and armour in the Czech Republic) and extensive collections of African and Native North American art. The collection known as the 'French Library', numbering around twelve thousand volumes and including valuable works in the field of Bohemian studies, was brought here from Paris.

Thanks to its richly furnished historical interiors and valuable collections, Opočno can rightly be considered the renaissance treasure house of East Bohemia.

OSTRAVA

Monument to the Industrial Revolution

IN THE MID-NINETEENTH CENTURY the Ostrava Region (now the Moravian-Silesian Region), where the monumental structures of mining headframes, blast furnaces, factory buildings and chimneys are an inseparable part of the landscape, became one of the most important industrial centres of the Austrian Empire. Its development was also accelerated by the presence of the railway. Emperor Ferdinand's company Severní dráhy (Northern Railway), supported by capital from the Rothschild banking house, obtained the licence to construct and expand this railway. Its purpose was to create a backbone connection between Vienna and Kraków, primarily for the transport of salt from the mines at Bochnia and Wieliczka. Over time, however, most of the nearby railways came under the company's control, allowing an unprecedented volume of transport of raw materials, goods and passengers within the region. The necessary construction components were supplied by the Vítkovice Ironworks, also owned by the Rothschilds. Due to its high consumption of coal, the company bought the Michal Coalmine (Důl Michal) in Michálkovice, Silesia in 1856.

The original state mine, named after the imperial privy counsellor Michael Laier, was connected to the railway network in 1862, and was later to transport the output of several neighbouring mines. The

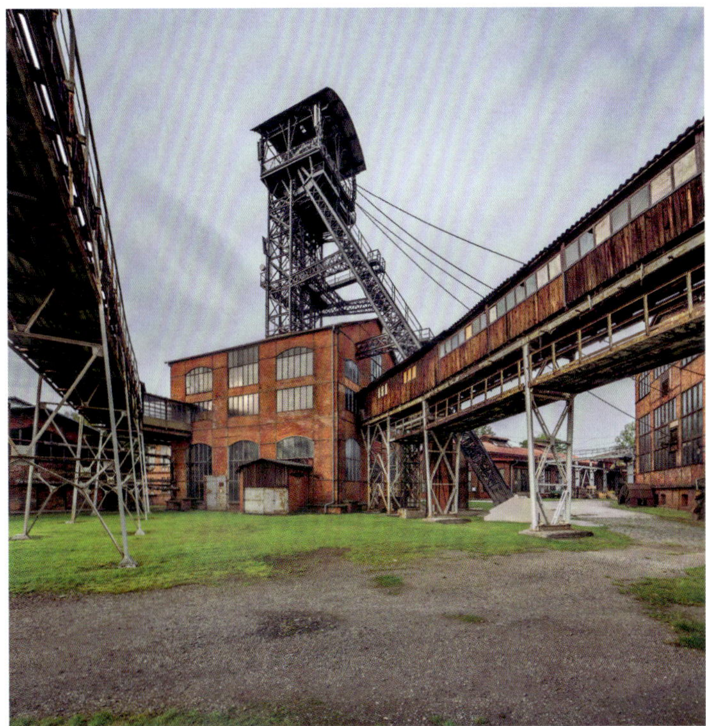

company's growing prosperity made it possible to undertake a large-scale rebuilding project in 1912–15 according to a plan by the Ostrava architect František Fiala, a pupil of Otto Wagner, renowned professor at the Vienna Academy of Fine Arts. The administrative buildings gained fairfaced brick façades and Secession elements, and the newly electrified mining installations also underwent radical modernisation. The interiors were fitted out with large-capacity changing rooms and washrooms for the miners, as well as offices for geologists and mining surveyors and other necessary departments.

Mining at the Michal Coalmine stopped in 1994. After these shafts had been filled in, the authentically preserved site was taken over by the National Heritage Institute, which manages it as a unique technology heritage site recalling Ostrava's industrial fame.

PERNŠTEJN

Impregnable marble castle

PERNŠTEJN CASTLE, MAJESTICALLY towering over a rock in the romantic landscape of the upper River Svratka, is a unique reminder of the age-old knightly history of the Lords of Pernštejn. The medieval magnates, who had an aurochs head on a silver field as their coat-of-arms, built the castle in the midst of countryside full of impenetrable woods at some point in the mid-thirteenth century. According to the fashion of the time, the magnates gave the castle the German name Bärenstein – bear stone.

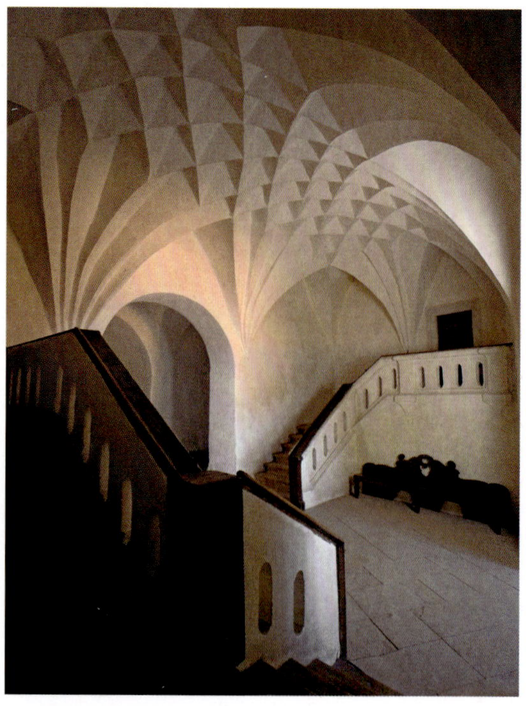

Over the centuries the Lords of Pernštejn became one of the most powerful Moravian dynasties, and their stronghold was equally mighty. Almost every Pernštejn left his mark on the castle; it underwent its greatest changes under Jan I of Pernštejn, when it gained its present form. The fortifications were altered with the addition of towers and gates, and the castle palace was also enlarged, with many oriel windows added, so that the castle's upper floors became larger in area than the ground plan. The main building material at that time was white Nedvědice marble, and as a result Pernštejn came to be known as the 'Marble Castle'. The magnificent residence is no less impressive after subsequent renaissance and baroque alternations.

Rebuilding in the seventeenth and eighteenth centuries took place under other owners, because the Lords of Pernštejn were forced to sell their ancient family seat in 1596. During the High Baroque one of these owners was Emperor Leopold I's personal physician, the imperial knight Franz Paul von Stockhamer, who had the castle rooms rebuilt, especially the impressive Knights' Hall, which became one of the most perfect baroque interiors in Moravia. In the early nineteenth century an *anglo-chinois* park was created on the slopes below the castle; this was embellished with several buildings and a number of statues, and has now been restored to its original form.

Pernštejn Castle, the pearl of Moravian castles, built in white Nedvědice marble, ranks among the best-preserved castles in the Czech Republic. Its late gothic and early renaissance features represent a highly individual transformation of a medieval fortress into a luxurious renaissance residence.

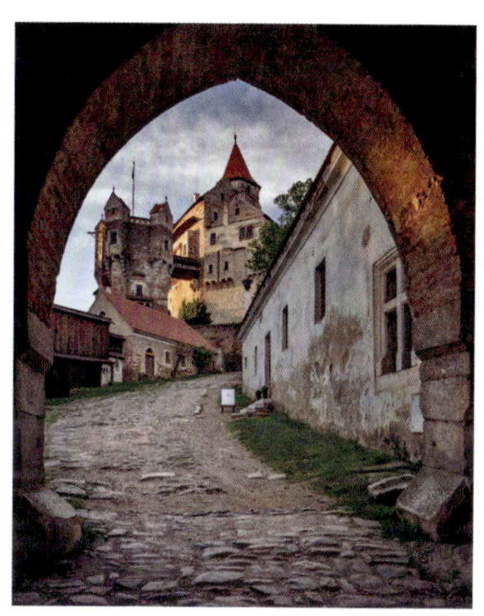

PLASY

Monastery

First Cistercian monastery in Bohemia –
Santini's art of building a monastery on water

THE FORMER CISTERCIAN MONASTERY in the valley of the River Střela was founded in 1144 by the Přemyslid prince Vladislaus II as the first Cistercian royal foundation; however, only parts of its medieval layout have survived. The Church of the Assumption of the Virgin Mary, rebuilt in the baroque style in 1661–66 by the eminent architect Jean Baptiste Mathey, stands on the original romanesque ground plan; its western front is marked by a unique, recently discovered romanesque portal. Of the former Přemyslid residence dating from the mid-thirteenth century, the two-storey Chapel of St Václav (Wenceslas) and St Mary Magdalene remains. This was later converted into the monastery's baroque granary, with a clocktower and a still-functioning clock mechanism dating from 1686.

The monastery site gained its present majestic appearance as a result of baroque rebuilding in 1661–1793 with the participation of the most eminent baroque master-builders and artists of Central Europe. The monastery building – the work of the architectural genius Jan Blažej

Santini-Aichel – stands on 5,100 oak stilts which serve to consolidate the underlying marshy ground. Water was directed to the bases of these stilts so that the wood would remain submerged without exposure to air, to prevent rotting. To this day the level, temperature and quality of the water are monitored four times daily. The ingenious water system is occasionally open to the public.

In 1785, during the Enlightenment reforms of Emperor Joseph II, the Cistercian monastery – the largest and most renowned in Bohemia – was dissolved. Forty years later it became the residence of Chancellor Klemens von Metternich and his family, who established their family tomb there. After the Second World War Metternich's property was nationalised. Today most of the impressive buildings are under the administration of the National Heritage Institute, which presents the monastery to visitors as a unique baroque heritage site of Central European importance, and a remarkable record of the building technologies of those times.

PRAGUE
Palace Gardens below Prague Castle

Historic oases of calm hidden in the heart of Prague

IN MEDIEVAL TIMES THE Prague palaces, located mainly in Prague Old Town, Hradčany and Malá Strana, were already part of the network of Bohemian aristocratic residences. In the Baroque period, they became the principal and most frequently used family seats, and this was often the stimulus for magnificent rebuilding projects involving the foremost Prague artists. When remodelling the buildings, the architects were faced with a lack of space, given that most of the palaces were located on medieval plots of land. This essentially ruled out the large-scale gardens which, as part of the baroque lifestyle, were as important as the palaces themselves. Gardens with summerhouses were therefore often laid outside the city walls, but were usually swallowed up in the fast-paced expansion of the suburbs in the nineteenth century.

In this respect, the gardens on the slopes beneath Prague Castle provide a unique record of the refined taste of the baroque aristocracy in Bohemia and an unrivalled example of baroque garden architecture. The interconnected terrace gardens, with their stairways, sale terrene, viewing points, greenhouses and statues, serve as an extension of the aristocratic palaces situated in today's Valdštejnská Street. The Small Fürstenberg, Kolowrat, Ledebour and Pálffy Gardens are now named after the last owners of the palaces, but in the eighteenth century the most prominent Czech aristocratic families, such as the Waldsteins, Czernins and Kolowrats, had them built as extensions to their homes.

The importance these families attached to their superb gardens can be seen in the choice of outstanding artists they invited to take part in their creation. These included the architects František Maxmilián Kaňka and Jan Nepomuk Palliardi, the painters Václav Vavřinec Reiner and Antonín Tuvora and a number of excellent sculptors. The gardens, restored at great cost and offering an unrivalled panoramic view of the city, are among the true pearls of the UNESCO-listed historic heart of Prague.

SLATIŇANY

Set in the heart of hunting country, a château steeped in equestrian lore

FROM 1746 ONWARDS THE small town of Slatiňany in East Bohemia, with its eponymous château and extensive country park, belonged to the Princes of Auersperg, for whom the intimacy and comfort of this small residence were more important than display and ostentation.

The château gained its present appearance after 1857, during the time of Prince Vincenz Karl von Auersperg, when, in the course of neo-gothic alterations, it was furnished with towers and extended with a wing serving as accommodation for guests from the nobility. On the model found in the highest social circles in England, these guests shared with the lord of the château a love of thoroughbred horses for hunting and racing. His son Prince Franz Joseph showed a similar passion for horses and did not hesitate to take on English trainers for the racehorses that regularly participated in the Grand Pardubice Steeplechase. This race first took place in 1874 and went down in horseracing history as one of the toughest races in Europe. New stable buildings were erected on the edge of the château park. At the time, these were among the most modern buildings of their kind owned by the monarchy,

and they are still used for breeding Old Kladruber black horses, an original
Czech breed specially reared for ceremonial purposes.

The prince had a children's farm set up in the château park, again on
the English model. The group of small wooden buildings served not only
as a playground but also for educating the princely scions, who gained
a grounding in natural history, the history and geography of the region,
and horticulture; they also learned about the care of livestock. Despite
their privileged status, they gained an awareness of the value of money
and human labour.

In recent years Slatiňany Château has undergone an exemplary historical restoration which emphasises the pervading atmosphere of this
welcoming, intimate aristocratic residence as it was at the turn of the
nineteenth and twentieth centuries.

SYCHROV

Château

A French flower on Czech soil

SYCHROV CHÂTEAU IN NORTH Bohemia is a unique example of a neo-gothic aristocratic residence. In 1690–93 the Lamotte de Frintropp family had a baroque château built – initially with a single wing, and with a chapel and a farmyard – on the site of a former fortress. The estate gained greater importance, however, after it was bought by the prominent French princely family of the de Rohans in 1820. In the 1830s the first owner from this family, Charles Alain Gabriel de Rohan, had the château enlarged into an impressive late classicist residence with six wings. Then, in 1847, his nephew Camille Joseph Philippe Idesbald de Rohan

began an extensive programme of rebuilding in the then-fashionable romantic neo-gothic style. Massive towers were added to the château, and the interiors and exterior reflected the antiquity and renown of the French dynasty, which had settled in the territory of the Habsburg monarchy as a result of the French Revolution. The rebuilding took place under the supervision of the architect Josef Pruvot with the collaboration of a number of Czech artists, outstanding among whom was the talented wood carver Petr Bušek. His coffered ceilings, wall panelling and furniture gave the château's interiors a unique appearance which is still admired today. A large amount of space was assigned to the de Rohans'

portrait gallery, which included more than 240 works. This collection of French portraiture records prominent members of the immediate family and their relatives, including French kings, notably Louis XIV. Also noteworthy is the park with its unique range of trees, which was enlarged by Prince Camille in the style of English gardens. The château is also associated with frequent visits by the prominent composer Antonín Dvořák.

The château has been state-owned since 1945 and is open to the public, providing a comprehensive insight into life at the summer residence of a distinguished princely family in the second half of the nineteenth century.

ŠVIHOV

Castle

Fortress on the water

ŠVIHOV, LYING IN THE valley of the River Úhlava in West Bohemia, is an exceptionally well-preserved water castle with mighty defences, whose technical and fortification elements were progressively put to use in the sixteenth century. The combination of various bodies of water in the surrounding area – the river, its blind arms, artificial raceways and large artificial ponds in the valley floodplain – made it an impregnable stronghold. It was built on the site of an older castle in the late fifteenth century on

the orders of Půta Švihovský, a leading statesman, judge and diplomat of the Kingdom of Bohemia. He had the old castle converted into a residence befitting the times, with two palaces, a chapel, monumental entrance tower and massive inner and outer defences protected by moats. His work was completed by his son Jindřich in around 1520, employing the services of the royal builder Benedikt Ried (Rejt), who by that time had already completed work on the ceremonial halls and fortifications of Prague Castle.

Since the time of the late gothic rebuilding of Švihov, only fragments have survived from the original decoration and furnishing of the interiors. These are testimony to the high ambitions of the owner, for example the statues of Church Fathers from the castle chapel, dating from around 1489, and the murals in the Red Bastion (paintings of knightly tournaments, a pair of wrestlers, banquets and what appears to be a scene from ancient mythology depicting the Judgment of Paris).

The overall appearance of the completed castle site can be imagined from the authentic murals which were painted in the castle chapel after 1500 by an unknown artist. A monumental painting showing Saint George slaying the dragon includes a realistic representation of the newly built water castle set in an imaginary landscape.

Visitors today can also experience the special atmosphere of Švihov Castle at water level by taking one of the boat tours on the moat.

TELČ
Château

Renaissance jewel of the Vysočina Region

THE CHÂTEAU IS THE dominant architectural feature of the picturesque historic town centre of Telč, not far from the south-west border between Moravia and Bohemia, in the Vysočina Region. The historic centre of Telč ranks among the Czech Republic's most valuable urban monument reservations and therefore earned a place, together with the château, on the UNESCO World Heritage List in 1992.

The current state of the château, which extends above a meander of the Telč stream, is mainly the result of extensive alterations which were undertaken on the site of an older, fourteenth-century castle by Zacharias of Hradec, descended from the prominent aristocratic family of the Lords of Hradec. He drew his inspiration directly from renaissance Italy, where he travelled in 1551–52 in the company of other Bohemian and Moravian nobles, to greet the future king of Bohemia, Maximilian II von Habsburg.

Zacharias of Hradec began to realise his 'Italian dream' immediately after his return from Italy, and his wife, Catherine of Waldstein, played a part in this; the result was the dramatic transformation of the gothic castle into a luxurious renaissance residence, under the influence of the Italian renaissance. First, he rebuilt the 'Old Palace', as it was known, enriching it with new renaissance art. The vaulted halls on the ground floor, and the Banqueting Hall and Treasure House, for example, have been preserved to this day; they are decorated with figurative, mock-architectural sgraffito, which at the time was an entirely new technique in Bohemia. Then the construction of the North Palace began, where the Italian renaissance in its Telč manifestation developed to its full glory, most splendidly in the ceremonial halls of the palace. From the outset the Gold Hall, Blue Hall, Imperial Hall and so on must have astonished visitors with their grandiose scale and artistic decoration, which was especially evident on the opulent coffered ceilings decorated with richly carved reliefs.

The transformation of Telč Château continued with the construction of the South Palace and an arcade on the main courtyard, the laying out of a new garden and, above all, the spectacular rebuilding of the château's All Saints Chapel. This is where Zacharias of Hradec and his wife finally found their place of eternal rest. The chapel is dominated by the tomb, on the top slab of which the married pair are shown with hands joined in prayer, both of them looking eternally upwards to the vaulted chapel ceiling with its stucco relief on the theme of Ezekiel's vision of the resurrection of the dead.

In comparison with the fate of other château residences in the Czech Republic, Telč Château also has the advantage that it was never sold, but was exclusively inherited from dynasty to dynasty. This explains why subsequent generations of owners always approached the management of the château with an understanding of, and reverence for, the legacy of Zacharias of Hradec. As long ago as the nineteenth century, respectful repair and restoration of the site began, and the interiors of the château, once Zacharias's residence, gained additions in the form of objects associated with other aristocratic dynasties who, for a time, made Telč their

home. Numerous portraits, inlaid furniture and rare textiles recall the glorious past of Telč Château and its owners. The impressive interiors are complemented by the uniquely well-preserved exteriors of the buildings enclosing three courtyards, as well as a French garden bounded by arcaded wings and an extensive English park with a large orangery.

The château was nationalised after the Second World War, and the current administration of the National Heritage Institute follows on from the museological tradition of the last owners, the family of the counts of Podstatzky-Lichtenstein. A sign of this is the fact that the former guest accommodation in the château was converted into a museum in 2023, displaying a number of unique objects that had been hidden in the château's depositories for many decades. Thanks to the new exhibition the age-old story of the dynastic and local tradition continues to be preserved and elaborated.

VALTICE
Château

Residence of the Princes of Liechtenstein

VALTICE IN SOUTH MORAVIA is known today as the family seat of the Princes of Liechtenstein and, together with the nearby château of Lednice and the surrounding landscaped area, it creates a single historical site with UNESCO World Heritage status.

Valtice owes its fame to Prince Karl I von Liechtenstein. Under his direction the original castle, enlarged with a renaissance courtyard, was remodelled in mannerist style, evidently according to a plan by the imperial architect Giovanni Mario Filippi. The enlargement of the château was continued by his son Karl Eusebius, who rebuilt it in grandiose late baroque style and, within its rooms, established one the largest art collections in Central Europe.

The residence gained its present appearance in the early eighteenth century during the reign of Prince Anton Florian von Liechtenstein. He had the château remodelled according to a plan by the Viennese architect Anton Ospel, whose imprint is seen in the high Roman baroque style. Prince Joseph Johann Adam then enlisted the services of the decorative painter and theatre engineer Antonio Beduzzi, who decorated the façades and interiors of the château in the refined style that was admired in the imperial palace in Vienna. In the 1720s a richly decorated family chapel was built at the château; it is considered one of the most perfect baroque interiors in Central Europe. During the second

half of the eighteenth century Prince Aloys I commissioned a theatre hall in the château and an *anglo-chinois* garden. His brother Prince Johann I devoted much attention to the surroundings of the château, adding the Rendez-Vous summerhouse in the form of a triumphal arch, as well as a memorial colonnade.

Although only a fraction of the château's interior furnishing remained after the Second World War, the sumptuous rooms, together with the large collection of paintings, remain a testimony to the former prominence of the Princes of Liechtenstein.

VELHARTICE

Medieval castle linked by a stone bridge

VELHARTICE IS STILL A REMINDER of the complex construction history of this aristocratic castle in south-west Bohemia. The predominantly medieval castle lies at the edge of the Šumava mountain range near the German border and forms a prominent feature in the landscape, offering unrivalled views of the surrounding countryside. Its most striking architectural feature comprises the ruins of the palace known as Rajský

dům (Paradise House) and the Putna Tower, connected by a unique stone bridge, which is an original defensive element and the only one of its kind in Central Europe.

The castle, founded at the turn of the thirteenth and fourteenth centuries, enjoyed its greatest flowering when it served as the family seat of Bušek the Elder and Bušek the Younger of Velhartice, who were privy counsellors and chamberlains to the king of Bohemia and Holy Roman emperor Charles IV of Luxembourg. Models for the appearance of Velhartice can be seen in the castle architecture of medieval France, which Bušek often visited with Charles IV.

The castle became the focus of attention in the Kingdom of Bohemia in the mid-fifteenth century, when it was owned by the prominent royal official and Keeper of the Bohemian Crown Jewels Menhart of Hradec (Meinhard von Neuhaus). He opposed Jiří z Poděbrad, a contender for the Bohemian throne, and to stop his rise to power concealed the crown jewels in Velhartice Castle. In the seventeenth century Velhartice Castle and its estate were acquired by the imperial general Martin de Hoeff-Huerta, who had a new late renaissance palace built on the upper courtyard. The remaining parts of this include a picturesque two-storey arcade loggia providing breathtaking views of the Šumava mountain range. The former castle brewery, surviving in reconstructed form, forms part of the castle site. In the outer bailey there is an open-air museum of vernacular architecture with buildings transferred from the Šumava foothills.

VELKÉ LOSINY

Renaissance under misty mountain ramparts

AT THE FOOT OF the Hrubý Jeseník mountains stands one of the residences of the once influential and wealthy family of the Lords of Žerotín. On the site of an earlier fortress, a three-winged renaissance château was built before the end of the sixteenth century, with an arcaded courtyard and an octagonal tower with sgraffito decoration on the façades. Shortly after this was completed, a single-storey facing wing was built, in which the owners progressively concentrated the living quarters and the rooms used for social events. As a result the interiors of the high castle have been preserved in an exceptionally authentic form, hardly rivalled in the Czech Republic or anywhere in Europe.

Visitors to the château can admire the renaissance inlaid doors, windows with lens-like cast-glass panes and parquet floors. The original furnishings include a tiled stove dating from about 1585, carved silver chandeliers and a painted credenza with ornate protective rail, the only one of its kind in the Czech Republic. The walls in the château halls are decorated with leather relief and textile wall coverings dating from the seventeenth century, and Brussels and French tapestries. Also noteworthy are the Žerotíns' family portrait gallery, a collection of Dutch genre paintings and the oldest preserved volumes of the Žerotín library, kept in the original wooden lattice cupboards.

The Velké Losiny Château and estate were also notorious as the scene of the great witchcraft and heresy trials which took place in the second half of the seventeenth century, as commemorated in the château by contemporary documents.

In 1802 the Princes of Liechtenstein bought the château from the Žerotíns and used it as their summer residence. New social salons were added to the château interiors, in a harmonious, refined design in the Viennese Biedermeier style, as well as modern facilities in the form of a kitchen, bathroom and toilets.

Despite all the later alterations, it was pre-eminently the renaissance that left its mark on the château, making it one of the most beautiful examples of Moravian renaissance architecture.

VELTRUSY

Château

'Maison de plaisance' – a rural retreat

AFTER ENLARGEMENT AND REDECORATION of the interiors, the original baroque hunting lodge of Veltrusy became a perfect example of
a French-inspired rural retreat, or *maison de plaisance*, in Bohemia.
The rebuilding was undertaken by Rudolf, Count Chotek of Chotkow
and Wognin, son of the château's founder, who later became the State
Chancellor of the Monarchy and whose visitors included the Empress
Maria Theresa of Habsburg.

The remarkable building with a ground plan in the
form of a Saint Andrew's cross, designed in the early
eighteenth century by the Italian architect Giovanni
Alliprandi, was painted in the second half of the eighteenth century with rococo and chinoiserie themes to
complement the original baroque frescoes. The walls
were decorated with costly silk wallpapers imported
from China and France. The salons and apartments on
the *piano nobile* (main floor) were refurbished with the
addition of fireplaces with mirrors, crystal lights, rococo
tables, sofas and stately portraits of Empress Maria
Theresa, Emperor Franz Stephan and their children.

The French garden laid out in the surrounding countryside, encircled by the River Vltava and a canal, was
embellished with baroque sculptures. The château was
long known by the name of 'Insel' ('Island') because of its
position. Canopied boats, manned by boatmen in colour-
ful costumes, offered rides on the canal. When the imperial couple with
their retinue visited in 1754, Rudolf Chotek organised not only celebrations but also displays of products from the Kingdom of Bohemia. The
royal guests and their courtiers were able to purchase these at shops
located in the château and garden.

At the turn of the eighteenth and nineteenth centuries the chancellor's nephew and heir, Johann Rudolf Chotek, laid out a substantial country park over a wide area of the surrounding countryside, embellished with a number of romantic and historicising buildings. Since then the château complex, one of the masterpieces of the High Baroque and Rococo periods in Bohemia, has survived in this form with only minor changes.

VIZOVICE

Château

Family treasure house of art collections

THE ENLIGHTENMENT REFORMS of the Viennese court during the reign of Empress Maria Theresa enabled families of lower birth to rise in society; the members of these families could now occupy high positions at regional or state level on the strength of their abilities. Among them were the von Blümegen counts, associated with the château at Vizovice.

The estate with a small baroque château, built on the site of a medieval Cistercian monastery, was acquired in 1746 by the Canon of the Olomouc Chapter, later Bishop of Hradec Králové, Count Hermann Hannibal von Blümegen, who shortly afterwards began construction of the new château here. His brothers – the Austrian chancellor Count Heinrich Kajetan and the Moravian *Landeshauptmann* (*zemský hejtman* or governor) Johann Christoph – were also involved in the project, since the château was intended mainly for their descendants. The building was designed by the Brno architect and building contractor Franz Anton Grimm, who had travelled as a young man in Italy and France, where he carefully studied the châteaux, palaces and churches. He designed the château at Vizovice in accordance with French taste in an elegant rococo classicist style with regularly divided interiors, at the centre of which was a large salon with a rococo fresco.

Almost all members of the family in the eighteenth and early nineteenth century were buying works of art which they brought together at Vizovice, creating one of the most impressive art collections in Moravia, which perfectly reflects the taste of the aristocracy in the Enlightenment era.

In the early nineteenth century the château was inherited by the family of the von Stillfried counts, who treated their forebears' legacy with great respect. The last aristocratic owners even settled in the basement and only showed the rooms on the *piano nobile* (main floor) to the most distinguished guests. Thanks to them, the château at Vizovice has been preserved almost completely intact from the second half of the eighteenth century.

VRANOV NAD DYJÍ

Château

Majestic architecture in unspoilt countryside

IN 1687 THE ARCHITECT Johann Bernhard Fischer returned to Vienna after his prolonged period of study and work in Rome and Naples, where he became familiar with the new artistic forms of the High Baroque and is said to have acquired professional skills at the workshop of the Italian master Gian Lorenzo Bernini. One of his first clients was the imperial count Michael Johann II von Althann, owner of the Vranov estate in South Moravia with its ancient castle over the River Dyje, recently damaged by fire.

At the end of a high rocky promontory, on the site of a tower-like gothic chapel, the monumental oval Hall of Ancestors was built in 1688–95 and was to become the dominant feature of the château, which was conceived as a grand aristocratic residence. The main purpose of the hall with its outstanding artistic decoration was to underline the antiquity and honour of the Althann dynasty, originally from Bavaria, who were active as military leaders, diplomats and officials in the service of the Holy Roman emperors. The more than life-sized statues of ten of the most renowned ancestors, from the workshop of the Austrian sculptor Tobias Kracker, line the circumference of the hall. This ambitious design concept of a celebration of the House of Althann culminates in a magnificent fresco spanning the entire dome by another outstanding baroque artist, Johann Michael Rottmayr.

In addition to the impressive hall, Fischer designed the Chapel of the Most Holy Trinity at Vranov, complete with an underground family vault. Later alterations left their mark in the main living quarters, where the interiors were fitted out in the emerging style of neoclassicism. The constant alterations in the name of family status demanded huge expenditure which in the late eighteenth century completely drained the counts' treasury; the estate was sold by auction on the instigation of the creditors.

Nevertheless the magnificent hall of Vranov Château, majestically overlooking the unspoilt landscape of Podyjí National Park, recalls the former glory of the Althanns.

ZVÍKOV

A royal castle at the confluence of rivers

THE SOUTH BOHEMIAN CASTLE of Zvíkov at the confluence of the rivers of Vltava and Otava is rightly known as the king of Czech castles. It was built in the first half of the thirteenth century as a fortress and symbol of the might of the first Bohemian kings of the Přemyslid dynasty. Later, in the fourteenth century, Emperor Charles IV included it in the select group of 11 royal castles that must never be sold. Ultimately this intention was not fulfilled, and from the fifteenth century onwards the castle was owned by a succession of leading aristocratic families. The last of these were the Schwarzenbergs, who owned the castle until the mid-twentieth century. In 1948 the castle passed into state ownership and was opened to the public. The last major intervention affecting the castle was the filling of the Orlík Reservoir in the early 1960s, which submerged the fortified settlement under the castle with the Church of St Nicholas. The level of the rivers under the castle is now 40 metres higher.

The oldest castle building, known as the Hlíza Tower, was built with massive, rough-hewn blocks called *hlízy*, from which it took its name. The royal palace is the central

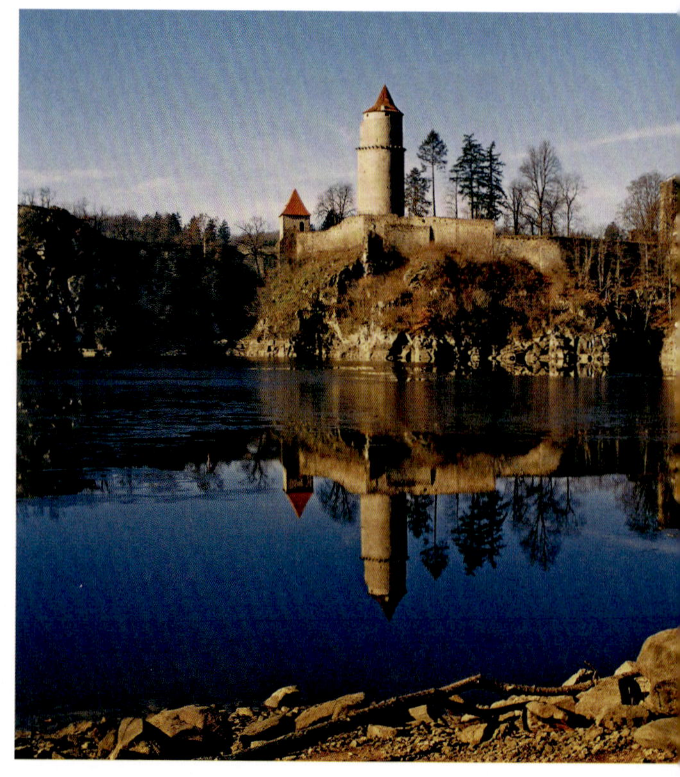

and most precious part of the castle area. Its enclosed courtyard is surrounded by arcaded galleries which served ceremonial functions and allowed easy access between individual sections of the palace. The most important of these after the royal chambers was the castle chapel, built in the classic gothic style of the time of King Louis IX of France, and it has been preserved intact to this day.

Although Zvíkov has had a complex history and has undergone many alterations, it remains one of the key buildings of Bohemian medieval secular architecture. Thanks to the royal palace, which has been preserved intact, it is also one of the foremost examples of the mature courtly art and architecture of the Bohemian royal dynasty of the Přemyslids.

ŽLEBY

Château

The Auerspergs' romantic vision of the Middle Ages

ONLY A HANDFUL OF HISTORIC buildings in the Czech Republic match the image of a romantic aristocratic residence as convincingly as Žleby Château in Central Bohemia. The original medieval castle on a promontory above the River Doubrava, rebuilt as a renaissance château with arcaded courtyards and remodelled in the Late Baroque period, underwent a magnificent neo-gothic transformation in 1847–65 which almost completely concealed the earlier iterations. The initiator of this major change was Prince Vincenz Karl von Auersperg, a member of one of the most prominent families of the Habsburg monarchy, who made Žleby Château his principal family seat in Bohemia in the mid-eighteenth century.

In accordance with his wishes, the existing comfortable château was transformed into an embodied evocation of a fortified castle of the High Middle Ages, with towers, gates, portcullises and ramparts, on the basis of a plan by the architects Benedikt Škvor and František Schmoranz. The prince drew his inspiration for this radical project during a visit to Britain in 1837, and from popular pattern books illustrating architectural and interior details of English aristocratic residences of the Tudor and Stuart eras. The château's interiors were also transformed. The airy rococo salons with fine white stucco were replaced by knights' halls, grand chambers and rooms with coffered ceilings, panelling, sgraffito plasterwork and leather wall coverings, filled with rare antiquities. Period replicas with a purely decorative function can be found here, in addition to the unique collection of painted glass windowpanes, renaissance weapons and armour, collections of baroque glassware, faience and majolica, furniture and works of artistic craftsmanship from the fifteenth to the seventeenth century. The château also has a chamber theatre in which members of the princely family and their friends performed favourite historical pieces in period costumes, intoxicated by the vision of a perfect Middle Ages which enchants visitors to this day.

Credits

Images

Front cover and back cover: © Libor Sváček

Front cover flap and back cover flap:
© National Heritage Institute of the Czech Republic

Inside pages: Archive of the National Heritage Institute,
Milan Bednařík, Ladislav Bezděk, Taťána Binková,
Gabriela Čapková, Gabriela Čočková, Martin Frouz,
Jan Gryc, Helena Heckelová, Radovan Kodera,
Karel Kuča, Pavel Macků, Hugo Moc, Michal Mráz,
Vladislav Razím, Josef Slavíček, Libor Sváček,
Věroslav Škrabánek, Miroslav Zavadil, Lukáš Zeman

Text

Lukáš Bojčuk, Marek Buš, Jiří Holub, Aleš Kadlčák,
Michal Konečný, Tomáš Kořínek, Ondřej Kubáček,
Eva Lukášová, Matěj Mejstřík, Jan Mikeš, Petr Pavelec,
Martin Rejman, Radek Ryšavý, Markéta Slabová,
Libor Švec, Petr Weiss

Map

Lukáš Hytha, Karel Kuča

FRONT COVER:
Lednice, Château
(pp. 46–49).

FRONT COVER FLAP:
Hluboká nad
Vltavou, Château
(pp. 20–21).

FRONTISPIECE:
Telč, Château
(pp. 76–79).

BACK COVER:
Vranov nad Dyjí,
Château (pp. 90–91).